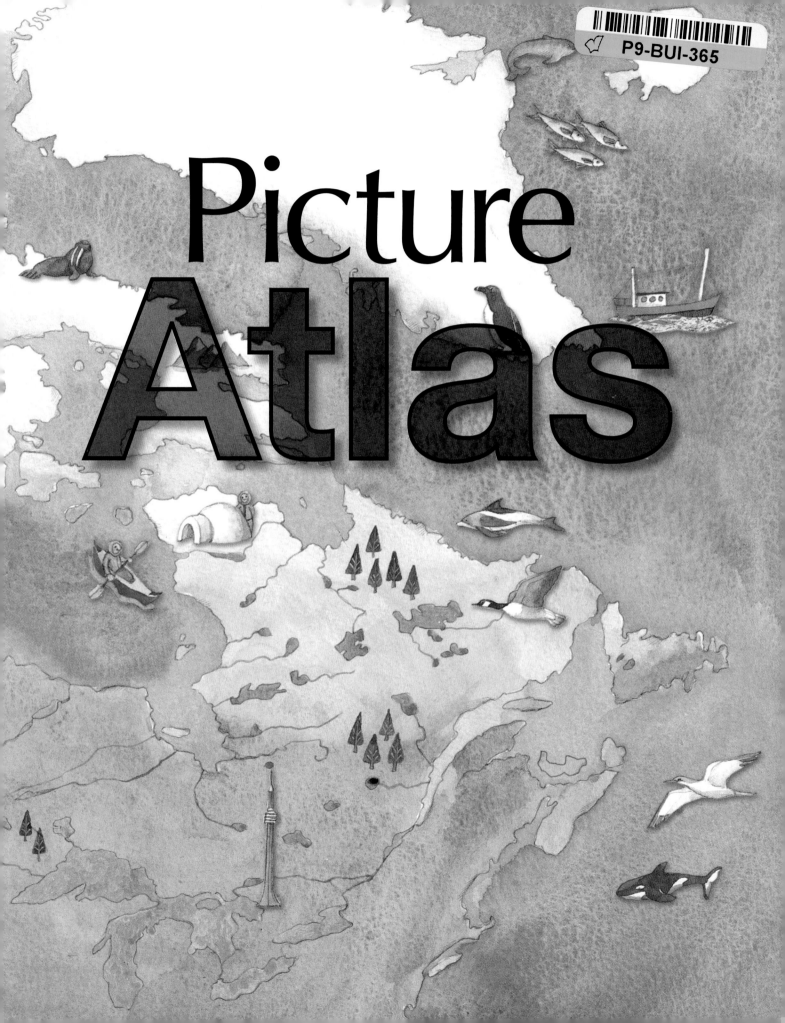

Picture
Atlas

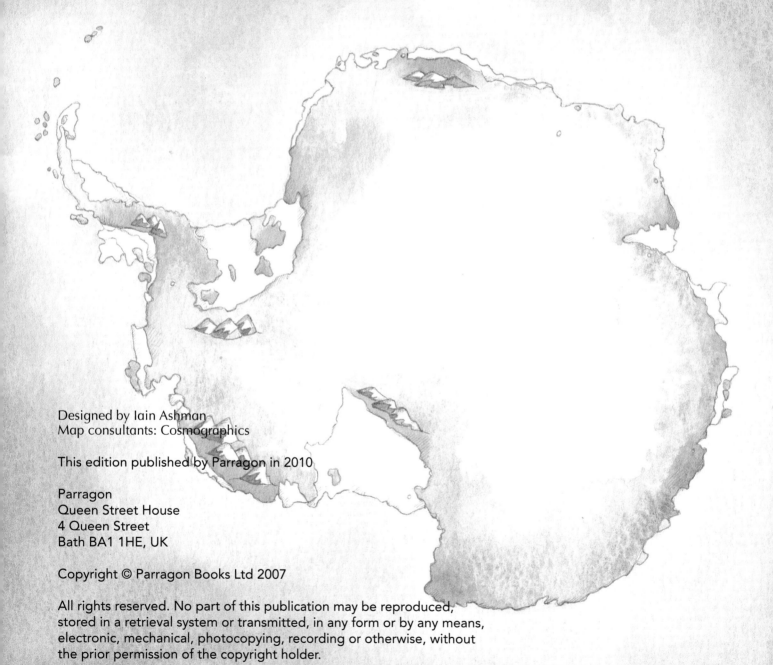

Designed by Iain Ashman
Map consultants: Cosmographics

This edition published by Parragon in 2010

Parragon
Queen Street House
4 Queen Street
Bath BA1 1HE, UK

ISBN 978-1-4075-8367-9

Printed in Indonesia

Picture Atlas

Illustrated by Helen Cann
Written by Pamela Beasant

PaRragon

Bath · New York · Singapore · Hong Kong · Cologne · Delhi · Melbourne

Contents

How the world works

Our world is an amazing place! It is the only planet we know about where people, animals, and plants can live. We can live here because we have water and sunlight, and can grow food and breathe the air.

What is the world made of?

The world is made mostly of rock. Toward the Earth's center (called the core) the rock melts because it is so hot. We live on a thin layer of land around the outside, called the crust.

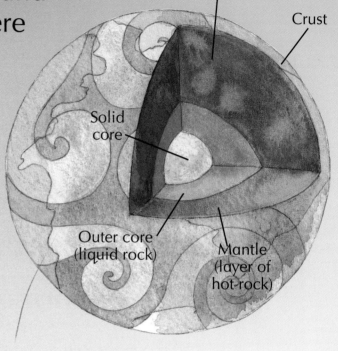

A diagram of how the world looks on the inside.

Crust

Solid core

Outer core (liquid rock)

Mantle (layer of hot-rock)

Plates

The Earth's crust is made up of giant pieces of rock called plates. The edges of the plates sometimes move against each other, causing earthquakes. Hot gas and rocks from under the crust sometimes explode through volcanoes.

Earth's crust

Most of the mountains in the world were pushed up millions of years ago when plates crashed together.

Mantle (hot rocks under the crust)

During eruptions hot rock called magma is pushed up from under the Earth's crust. When the magma cools, it forms new land.

Eruptions and earthquakes happen where two plates meet.

Hot and cold

The world spins around the Sun. It takes a year to go around once. The hottest parts of the world are nearest to the Sun. The coldest parts are at the very top and bottom, at the North and South Poles. They are farthest away from the Sun's heat.

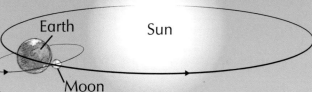

The Earth goes around the Sun, and the Moon goes around the Earth.

Earth   Sun   Moon

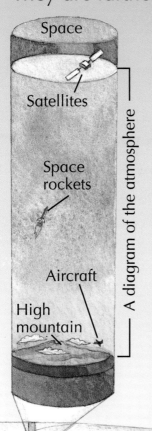

Space

Satellites

Space rockets

Aircraft

High mountain

A diagram of the atmosphere

The atmosphere

Around the Earth there is a layer of air called the atmosphere. It contains the oxygen we need to breathe. As it gets higher, the atmosphere becomes thinner until it disappears and space begins. That is why people who go into space have to take breathing equipment.

The atmosphere

How people live

People can live in most places in the world, but in some areas it is hard to survive. In very hot places, such as deserts, the Sun's heat can kill and there is often not enough to drink. In very chilly places the cold can be dangerous. For instance, people can only survive outside in the Antarctic if they wear a lot of protective clothing.

Weather

Weather is caused by the flow of air around the world. Storms happen when the air is moving very quickly. The worst storms are hurricanes—very strong winds that can do lots of damage.

DID YOU KNOW?

The world's water is recycled naturally. Water from the oceans, rivers, and lakes rises up (evaporates) into the air. It is carried around the world and falls back to Earth as rain.

9

How the world looks

The world looks very different depending on where you live. There are high mountains, wide rivers, massive forests, flat plains, and huge deserts. Some countries have good farm land, while others have little water and it is hard to grow food there. How people live partly depends on their country's weather and its landscape.

The highest mountains are the Himalayas in Asia.

The longest mountain range is the Andes in South America.

Mountains

Mountains are the highest things on Earth. They have been around for millions of years. A group of mountains in the same area is called a range.

Forests

The world's forests are very important because trees give out the oxygen we need to breathe, and provide us with wood. Tropical rainforests are forests that grow in warm wet areas of the world.

The biggest rainforest is Amazonia, South America.

Rivers

All rivers start small, high up in mountains or hills. As they flow across the land they become deeper and wider. They eventually flow into the sea.

The longest river is the Nile in North Africa.

Deserts

Deserts are huge areas of land that have very little water. Not much can grow in a desert and it is difficult to live there. Most deserts are hot, but some are cold.

Some animals and plants can survive well in deserts.

Desert people called nomads have the skills to live in desert lands.

Grasslands

Some countries have huge areas of flat, open grasslands. In North America this is called prairie. In South America it is the pampas, and in Russia it is called the steppe.

In Africa the grasslands are called the savanna. Lots of wild animals live there.

Countries

The world is divided into seven huge areas called continents. Each continent, (except for Antarctica) has lots of different countries in all shapes and sizes.

The smallest country is Vatican City, in Italy.

The biggest country is Russia.

Countries on the same piece of land have borders in between them. Borders are shown in red on the maps in this book.

Cities

Most countries have large cities, as well as smaller towns and villages. The main city is called the capital. On the maps in this book, capital cities are shown as blue squares.

DID YOU KNOW?

There are more than 190 countries, and over 3,000 different languages spoken in the world.

11

About maps

Maps show what places look like, seen from high above. They show the outline of a country or a town, and as much detail as possible about what the land is like and how it is used. Maps used to be made by people walking around studying the land. Now, photographs from satellites in space are used to make very accurate maps.

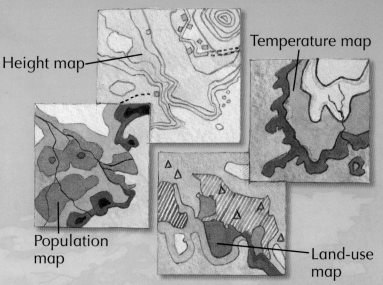

Height map

Temperature map

Population map

Land-use map

Picture maps

Maps can show different things. Some show how hot or cold a place is, or how high the land is. Others show what crops are grown, or how many people live there. The maps in this book are picture maps. They show places of interest, along with mini pictures.

Flat world

The world is a ball shape, and the best way to show an accurate map of the world is on a globe. In an atlas, a map of the world shows all the countries as if the world has been rolled out flat. It is not quite as accurate as a globe.

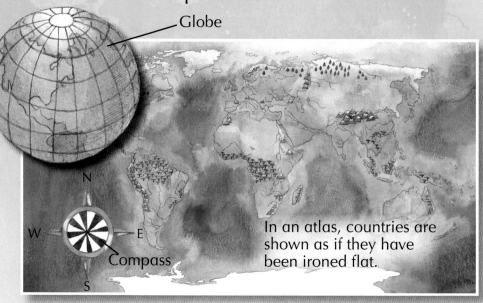

Globe

N
W   E
Compass
S

In an atlas, countries are shown as if they have been ironed flat.

North and south

Most maps have a compass that shows the direction of north, south, east, and west. There is a compass on every map in this book.

The Equator

Maps often show an imaginary line running around the middle of the world. This is called the Equator, which divides north from south. The climate near the Equator is much warmer and wetter than it is at the North and South Poles.

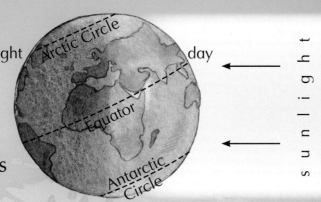

night · Arctic Circle · day · Equator · Antarctic Circle · sunlight

The lines showing the Arctic and Antarctic Circles mark the areas where days and nights last a very long time. For half the year, it is totally light, and for half the year the sun does not rise at all.

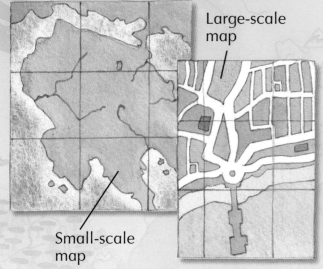

Large-scale map

Small-scale map

Big and small maps

Maps can show huge areas such as the whole world, or a small area such as one town. On a map of the world, a small distance represents many miles. Whether a map shows a big or a small area is called its "scale."

Map key

Map-makers use symbols to show things such as mountains and forests. Sometimes they explain what the symbols mean on the map. This is called a key.

The key to some of the symbols used on the maps in this book.	River	Pine forest
City	Lake	Country border
Capital city	Rainforest	Mountains

The world

The oceans surround the land we live on. The Pacific is the biggest and deepest ocean on earth. It covers about a third of the planet.

The seven continents are North America, South America, Asia, Africa, Europe, Australasia, and Antarctica.

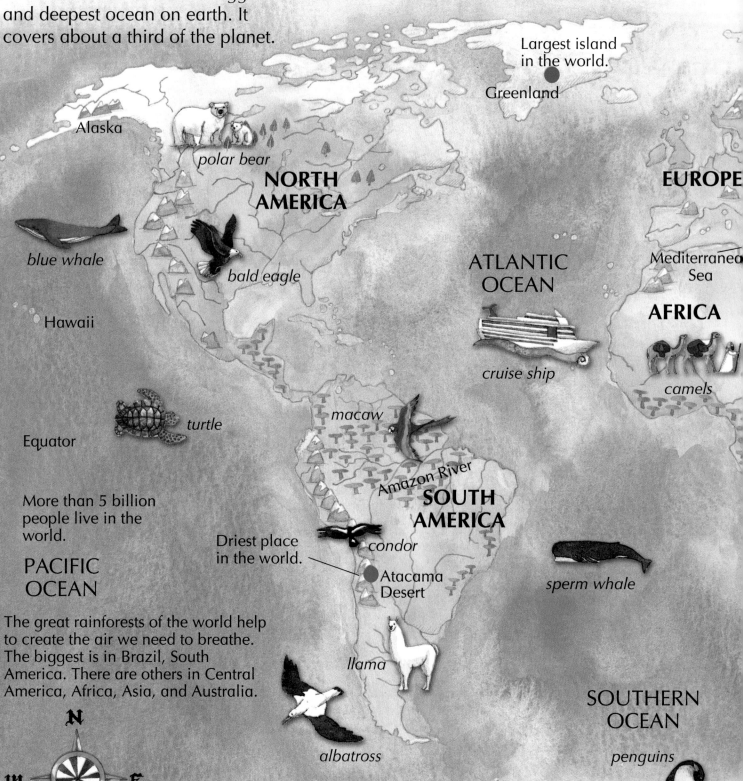

Largest island in the world. Greenland

Alaska

polar bear

NORTH AMERICA

blue whale

bald eagle

Hawaii

EUROPE

ATLANTIC OCEAN

Mediterranean Sea

AFRICA

cruise ship

camels

turtle

Equator

macaw

Amazon River

SOUTH AMERICA

Driest place in the world.

condor

Atacama Desert

sperm whale

More than 5 billion people live in the world.

PACIFIC OCEAN

The great rainforests of the world help to create the air we need to breathe. The biggest is in Brazil, South America. There are others in Central America, Africa, Asia, and Australia.

llama

SOUTHERN OCEAN

albatross

penguins

N
W   E
S

On land, the highest mountains are the Himalayas in Asia. Mount Everest is the highest peak.

There are great trenches under the oceans. The Marianas Trench in the Pacific is 35,820 ft deep.

The highest mountains on earth are under the sea. Mauna Loa is a mountain in the Pacific Ocean. Its peak sticks up out of the sea, forming an island. If it were uncovered, it would be higher than Mount Everest.

ARCTIC OCEAN

narwhal

reindeer

bear

ASIA

wolf

PACIFIC OCEAN

Biggest lake in the world.

giant panda

Caspian Sea

Highest place in the world.

Lowest place in the world.

snow leopard

Nile River

Dead Sea

Mount Everest

Deepest part of the oceans.

Longest river in the world.

Cherrapunji, India

Asian elephant

The Marianas Trench

Dalol, Ethiopia Hottest place in the world.

orangutan

great white shark

INDIAN OCEAN

Wettest place in the world.

ions

dolphins

lemurs

kangaroo

The great rivers are the lifelines of the continents. They provide water and carry people and goods across countries.

platypus

AUSTRALASIA AND OCEANIA

kiwi

Coldest place in the world.

fin whale

survey ship

Asia is the biggest continent. The smallest is Australasia.

Plateau Station

ANTARCTICA

15

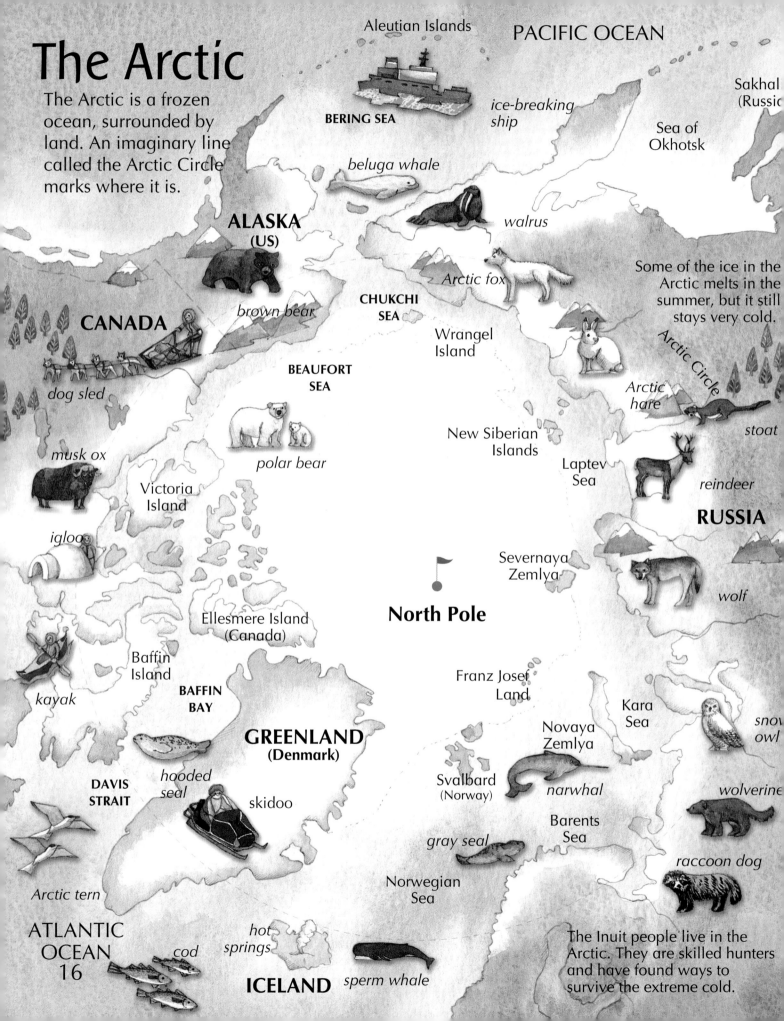

The Arctic

The Arctic is a frozen ocean, surrounded by land. An imaginary line called the Arctic Circle marks where it is.

Aleutian Islands

PACIFIC OCEAN

Sakhal (Russic

BERING SEA

ice-breaking ship

Sea of Okhotsk

beluga whale

walrus

ALASKA (US)

Arctic fox

Some of the ice in the Arctic melts in the summer, but it still stays very cold.

CANADA

brown bear

CHUKCHI SEA

Wrangel Island

Arctic Circle

Arctic hare

dog sled

BEAUFORT SEA

stoat

musk ox

polar bear

New Siberian Islands

Laptev Sea

reindeer

Victoria Island

RUSSIA

igloo

Ellesmere Island (Canada)

Severnaya Zemlya

North Pole

wolf

kayak

Baffin Island

BAFFIN BAY

Franz Josef Land

Kara Sea

snow owl

GREENLAND (Denmark)

Novaya Zemlya

hooded seal

DAVIS STRAIT

skidoo

Svalbard (Norway)

narwhal

wolverine

Barents Sea

gray seal

raccoon dog

Arctic tern

Norwegian Sea

ATLANTIC OCEAN
16

cod

hot springs

ICELAND

sperm whale

The Inuit people live in the Arctic. They are skilled hunters and have found ways to survive the extreme cold.

Antarctica

Antarctica is the coldest place on earth.
It is land covered by ice and snow.
Hardly anything can survive there.

No people live in Antarctica all
the time, but there are a few
scientific bases set up by different
countries. Scientists visit the bases
to do experiments.

ATLANTIC
OCEAN

survey ship

cod

elephant
seal

albatross

SOUTHERN OCEAN

blue
whale

South Orkney
Islands (UK)

Weddell
Sea

Queen
Maud
Land

tracked
vehicle

gentoo
penguin

weddell
seal

skidoo

Amery
Ice Shelf

Alexander
Island

Ronne
Ice Shelf

scientists

East
Antarctica

rockhopper
penguin

Ellsworth
Mountains
16,050 ft

South Pole

Queen
Mary
Land

blue-
eyed
shag

West Antarctica

polar
aircraft

krill

Ross
Ice Shelf

Wilkes
Land

Ross
Sea

emperor
penguin

leopard seal

PACIFIC
OCEAN

Antarctic Circle

chinstrap
penguin

Scientists think that the ice on
Antarctica is melting. If this
happens, the world's oceans will
get deeper and some of its land
will be covered in water.

fin
whale

SOUTHERN
OCEAN

The lowest
temperature ever
recorded was in
Antarctica. It was
-125.2°F.

17

Canada

Canada is a very big country. It has many high mountains and is very cold in winter. Parts of Canada are inside the Arctic Circle.

Arctic char

Ellesm
Islan

ALASKA (US)

Queen Elizabeth Islands

Banks Island

Beaufort Sea

beluga whale

polar bear

Prince of Wales Island

Arctic Circle

Mount McKinley

American black bear

Arctic hare

Victoria Island

great northern diver

muskrat

Great Bear Lake

skidoo

Whitehorse

snow goose

Canada has lots of oil under the ground that no one has ever used.

gray whale

Mackenzie River

Yellowknife

Great Slave Lake

logging

Rocky Mountains

woodchuck

Churchi

Lake Athabasca

Queen Charlotte Islands

totem pole

mounted police

beaver

Reindeer Lake

Edmonton

North American porcupine

Lake Winnipeg

salmon

Vancouver Island

Vancouver

Calgary

Victoria

PACIFIC OCEAN

Regina

Lake Manitoba

Winnipeg

wild turkey

monarch butterfly

sperm whale

The Rocky Mountains stretch down through the west of Canada.

UNITED STATES

18

Greenland is the biggest island in the world. It belongs to Denmark. Hardly anyone lives there.

Qaanaaq

harp seal

GREENLAND (DENMARK)

ICELAND

Reykjavik

narwhal

Iceland is part of Europe. It has lots of volcanoes and hot springs, called geysers.

Baffin Bay

walrus

bowhead whale

Arctic Circle

razorbill

herring

Baffin Island

Davis Strait

Nuuk

trawler

Foxe Basin

Canada is at the top of the North American continent. It is the second biggest country in the world.

cod

Southampton Island

Hudson Strait

white-beaked dolphin

The English and French languages are both spoken in Canada.

Hudson Bay

igloo

kayak

ATLANTIC OCEAN

Belcher Islands

CANADA

Canada goose

Newfoundland

St John's

St Lawrence River

Gulf of St Lawrence

Prince Edward Island

The Great Lakes are inland seas. They are joined to the Atlantic Ocean by the St Lawrence River.

Charlottetown

Fredericton

Halifax

gannet

Quebec

Nova Scotia

CN Tower

Montreal

N

Ottawa

Lake Superior

Toronto

W

E

killer whale

Lake Huron

Lake Ontario

Niagara Falls

Lake Michigan

Lake Erie

S

19

US

The United States (US) is divided into 50 states. There are mountains, forests, lakes, prairies, and deserts in different parts of the US.

killer whale

Seattle

Portland

giant redwood tree

red deer

wolf

Mount Rushmore

bald eagle

Rocky Mountains

Golden Gate Bridge

mountain goat

bison

rattlesnake

Salt Lake City

UNITED STATES

San Francisco
San José

CASINO

Denver

pronghorn

PACIFIC OCEAN

Las Vegas

Hollywood

Death Valley

Grand Canyon

Los Angeles

Colorado River

cactus

beef cattle

San Diego

Phoenix

rodeo

Hawaii (US)

surfing

Alaska and Hawaii are part of the US. Can you find them on the world map?

MEXICO

San Antonio

RUSSIA

ALASKA (US)

CANADA

fur seal

Mount McKinley

sea otter

The people who lived in America before it became the US are called Native Americans. There are different Native American tribes, such as the Sioux and the Navaho.

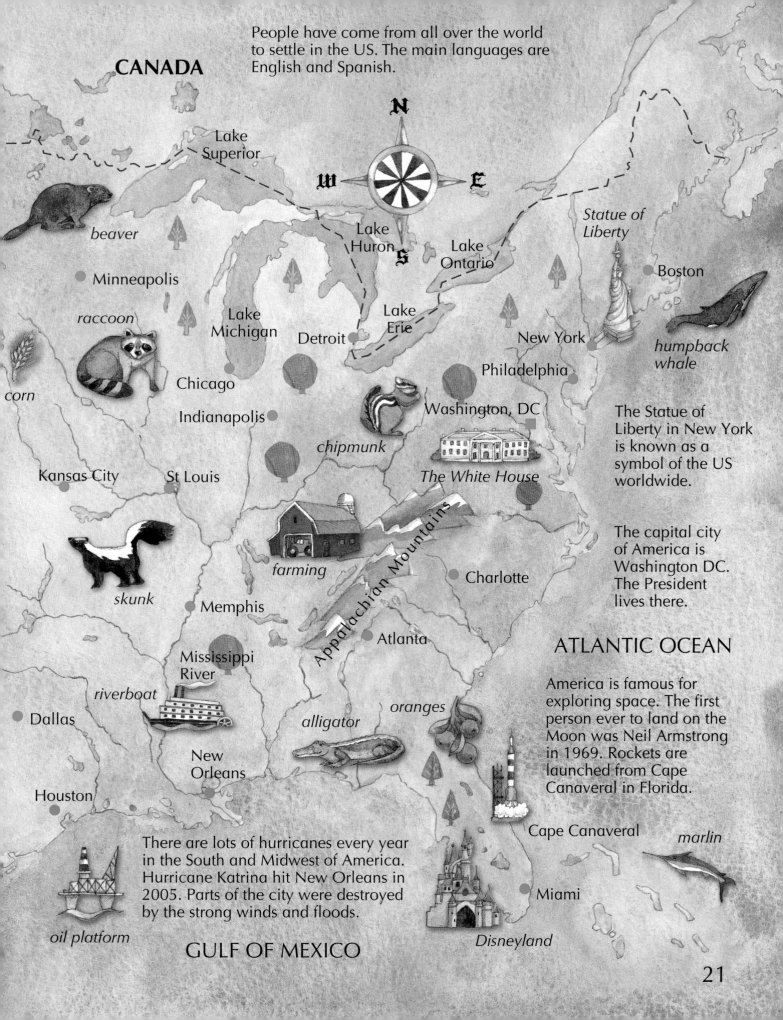

People have come from all over the world to settle in the US. The main languages are English and Spanish.

CANADA

N
W E
S

Lake Superior

Lake Huron

Lake Ontario

Statue of Liberty

Boston

beaver

Minneapolis

raccoon

Lake Michigan

Detroit

Lake Erie

New York

humpback whale

Philadelphia

corn

Chicago

Indianapolis

Washington, DC

chipmunk

The Statue of Liberty in New York is known as a symbol of the US worldwide.

Kansas City

St Louis

The White House

skunk

farming

Charlotte

The capital city of America is Washington DC. The President lives there.

Memphis

Appalachian Mountains

Atlanta

ATLANTIC OCEAN

Mississippi River

riverboat

oranges

America is famous for exploring space. The first person ever to land on the Moon was Neil Armstrong in 1969. Rockets are launched from Cape Canaveral in Florida.

Dallas

alligator

New Orleans

Houston

Cape Canaveral

marlin

There are lots of hurricanes every year in the South and Midwest of America. Hurricane Katrina hit New Orleans in 2005. Parts of the city were destroyed by the strong winds and floods.

Miami

oil platform

GULF OF MEXICO

Disneyland

21

Central America and the West Indies

Mexicali

Tijuana

coyote

UNITED STATES

Rio Grande

Hermosillo

nine-banded armadillo

bobcat

MEXICO

Monterrey

Lots of hurricanes form in the Gulf of Mexico and move over the land, sometimes causing terrible damage.

GULF OF MEXICO

blue-footed booby

Culiacan

Toltec statue

Pyramid of the Sun

spectacled owl

Cancun

ring-tailed coati

Guadalajara

Mérida

oil

Chichen Itza

Revillagigedo Islands (Mexico)

Mexico City

Puebla

Veracruz

coffee

BELIZE

Belmopan

frigate bird

Mount Popocatepetl

Olmec carved head

The Spanish explorer Hernando Cortés sailed to Central America in search of gold. He landed in Mexico in 1519. The people who lived there, called the Aztecs, had a big empire. They were defeated by Cortés, and the empire was destroyed.

Acapulco

HONDURA

GUATEMALA

Tegucigalpa

Guatemala

San Salvador

sailing

EL SALVADOR

Managu

Mexico City is built on the ruins of the Aztec capital, Tenochtitlan.

NICARAGUA

San José

COSTA RICA

common dolphin

This narrow bridge of land was created by volcanoes many millions of years ago.

PACIFIC OCEAN

tuna

The Panama Canal connects the Pacific Ocean to the Atlantic. It is a shortcut for the ships, so that they don't have to sail around Cape Horn at the bottom of South America.

giant tortoise

The Galapagos Islands have lots of unusual birds and animals. The biologist, Charles Darwin, who first wrote that living things evolved (changed) over thousands of years, formed some of his ideas after visiting the islands.

GALAPAGOS ISLANDS (ECUADOR)

iguana

There are thousands of islands that make up the West Indies. Many of them are tiny with few or no people. The islands are the tops of a mountain range that lies under the sea.

diving

cruise ship

sailfish

NORTH ATLANTIC OCEAN

Cuvier's beaked whale

BAHAMAS

Nassau

—SAN SALVADOR

TURKS & CAICOS ISLANDS (UK)

PUERTO RICO (US)

VIRGIN ISLANDS (UK & US)

ANGUILLA (UK)

sugar cane

Havana

CUBA

pirate wrecks

ST MARTIN (FRANCE)

bee hummingbird (the world's smallest bird)

DOMINICAN REPUBLIC

HAITI

Port-au-Prince

Santo Domingo

San Juan

ANTIGUA & BARBUDA

JAMAICA

Kingston

GUADELOUPE (FRANCE)

CAYMAN ISLANDS (UK)

ST KITTS & NEVIS

DOMINICA

MONTSERRAT (UK)

CARIBBEAN SEA

MARTINIQUE (FRANCE)

ST LUCIA

ST VINCENT & THE GRENADINES

BARBADOS

tarpon

brown pelican

Port of Spain

GRENADA

TRINIDAD & TOBAGO

Panama Canal

flamingo

PANAMA

Orinoco River

bananas

Panama City

sun parakeet

GULF OF PANAMA

Christopher Columbus sailed west from Europe. He was trying to find an easier route to the rich countries of the east. He landed on San Salvador, in the Bahamas, in 1492, and thought that he had found India. This is why the islands were called the West Indies.

N
W   E
S

23

South America

South America covers a huge area. It has mountains, rainforests, and grassy plains, called pampas, that stretch for miles.

The main languages spoken in South America are Spanish, Portuguese, and English.

The Amazon River is the second longest river in the world.

Lake Titicaca is the highest lake in the world. It is 12,507 ft above sea level.

CARIBBEAN SEA

ATLANTIC OCEAN

Equator

oil tanker

oil platform

cruise ship

Maracaibo

Caracas

Medellín

Bogotá

Quito

VENEZUELA

COLOMBIA

ECUADOR

GUYANA

SURINAME

FRENCH GUIANA

Georgetown

Paramaribo

Cayenne

French rocket base

armadillo

Angel Falls (world's highest waterfall)

spectacled bear

Mount Cotopaxi

capybara

piranha fish

toucan

Belem

Amazon River

Manaus

sloth

giant anteater

Amazon river dolphin

squirrel monkey

jaguar

scarlet macaw

anaconda

BRAZIL

Brasília

Brasilia cathedral

manatee

Cape of Sao Roque

Recife

Fortaleza

scarlet ibis

Salvador

sardines

PERU

Lima

Machupicchu ruins

alpaca

La Paz

Mount Ancohuma

Lake Titicaca

BOLIVIA

24

ATLANTIC OCEAN

bottlenose dolphin

blue whale

ocelot

Rio de Janeiro

São Paulo

Statue of Christ in Rio de Janeiro

guinea pig

PARAGUAY

Asunción

falabella mini horse

Pôrto Alegre

mail ship

The rainforest in Brazil is the biggest one in the world. It is so thick in places that the sunlight does not reach the forest floor. It rains every day and sometimes the Amazon river floods.

Trees in the rainforest help to make the air we breathe. In places, however, the trees have been cut down to make room for growing crops. If the rainforest disappears it is likely to affect the planet's climate.

URUGUAY

Montevideo

River Plate

beef cattle

Buenos Aires

vampire bat

The Atacama Desert is the driest place on Earth.

chinchilla

Mount Aconcagua

Andes Mountains

shellfish

Santiago

CHILE

ARGENTINA

llama

Risso's dolphin

sardines

sheep

puma

leopard seal

fin whale

albatross

Falkland Islands (UK)

Stanley

South Georgia (UK)

The tip of South America is near Antarctica. It is very cold.

elephant seal

volcanoes

Tierra del Fuego

Cape Horn

The sea around Cape Horn is a very dangerous place for ships. It has strong currents and violent storms.

SOUTHERN OCEAN

PACIFIC OCEAN

The Incas lived in Peru hundreds of years ago. They built an empire which stretched over Chile and Ecuador. The Incas worshipped the sun and nature gods. Lots of people visit the ruins of Machu Picchu, one of the cities where the Incas lived.

The Andes are the longest mountain range in the world. Some people live high in the mountains. They use llamas to carry loads up the narrow mountain paths.

25

Western Europe

Europe is made up of a lot of different countries. In the past, European countries controlled many lands far away from Europe. They still govern some faraway islands, called "territories."

A warm ocean current called the Gulf Stream runs from North America, past Europe and into the Arctic Circle. If it wasn't there, the sea around northern Europe would be much colder and the winters longer and harder.

Parts of Europe in the far north are very cold. The upper areas of Norway, Sweden, and Finland are all inside the Arctic Circle.

Much of Europe has a mild climate, which means the weather is not extremely hot or cold all the time.

reindeer

Hammerfest

Tromso

Kiruna

Narvik

snowy owl

Gulf of Bothnia

FINLAND

Helsinki

Tallinn

ESTONIA

Riga

LATVIA

Vilnius

LITHUANIA

Part of RUSSIA

Kaliningrad

Warsaw

white stork

POLAND

Gdansk

Poznan

Berlin

SWEDEN

Stockholm

Uppsala

Lake Vanern

Gotland

Gothenburg

historic ships

Baltic Sea

Malmo

Copenhagen

Hamburg

Brandenburg Rhine Gate

Amsterdam

Norwegian Sea

cod

Trondheim

NORWAY

stavekirk

Bergen

Oslo

DENMARK

North Sea

ferry

NETHERLANDS

Tower Bridge

London

cuckoo wrasse

fishing boat

Arctic Circle

ICELAND

eider duck

Reykjavik

Faroe Islands (Denmark)

Shetland Islands (UK)

puffin

Aberdeen

Edinburgh

Glasgow

Belfast

Liverpool

Dublin

Birmingham

Cardiff

UNITED KINGDOM

IRELAND

Stonehenge

Rockall

ATLANTIC OCEAN

Orkney Islands (UK)

Western Isles (UK)

golden eagle

Northern Ireland (UK)

cattle

basking shark

26

Krakow

SLOVAKIA

Bratislava

Budapest

CZECH REP.

Prague

HUNGARY

Danube River

Belgrade

SERBIA

KOSOVO

Pristina

Skopje

Athens

GREECE

MACEDONIA

olive tree

Salzburg

Vienna

AUSTRIA

SLOVENIA

Ljubljana

Zagreb

CROATIA

Sarajevo

BOSNIA-HERZEGOVINA

Podgorica

MONTE-NEGRO

Tirana

ALBANIA

Black Forest

Munich

LUXEMBOURG

LIECHTENSTEIN

Bern

SWITZERLAND

Alps

Venice

gondola

Leaning Tower of Pisa

SAN MARINO

ITALY

Colosseum

Rome

Naples

Mount Vesuvius

Mount Etna

olive tree

Sicily (Italy)

MALTA

Valletta

seahorse

trumpetfish

The Mediterranean Sea is warm and quite shallow. It only has a narrow channel connecting it to the Atlantic Ocean. Because of this, it has hardly any tides at all.

grapes

FRANCE

Paris

Eiffel Tower

Lyons

Mont Blanc

Milan

wild horses

Marseilles

Corsica (France)

Sardinia (Italy)

Cagliari

octopus

Brest

Nantes

Loire River

Bordeaux

Garonne River

grapes

ANDORRA

Pyrenees

Barcelona

Balearic Islands

Ibiza

Minorca

Majorca

(Spain)

Mediterranean Sea

Southern European countries are very hot in the summer.

NORTH AFRICA

Most countries in Europe are part of a group called the European Union. Some of these countries now use the same currency (money) called the Euro.

(UK)

cruise ship

pilchards

Bay of Biscay

Vigo

Oporto

olive tree

PORTUGAL

Lisbon

River Tagus

Córdoba

Málaga

Gibraltar (UK)

Ceuta (Spain)

Bilbao

Pamplona

bulls

Madrid

SPAIN

flamenco dancers

Granada

anchovies

N   E   S

W

27

Eastern Europe

Barents Sea

Arctic Circle

ice-breaking
ship

Arctic fox

This part of Europe
contains many countries.
In the far north the
climate is very cold.
Down in the south the
climate is much warmer.

Ural Mountains

elk

brown bear

gray wolf

The Volga is
Europe's
longest river.

Arkhangelsk

White
Sea

osprey

Lake Onega

Lake Ladoga

In 1917, there was a revolution in Russia and the
king (called the Czar) and his family were killed.
The country was ruled by the communist party
until 1991. It now has an elected president.

Volga River

St Basil's
Cathedral

Moscow

Murmansk

Hammerfest

reindeer

Sami reindeer
herders

snowy owl

NORWAY

SWEDEN

FINLAND

Gulf of Bothnia

Vaasa

Tampere

Helsinki

Gulf of Finland

Tallinn

Stockholm

Uppsala

Lake Vanern

Gotland

mountain
hare

historic ships

Baltic
Sea

Malmo

St Petersburg

Winter Palace

RUSSIA

badger

Smolensk

BELARUS

Minsk

ESTONIA

LATVIA Riga

LITHUANIA Vilnius

RUSSIA

Kaliningrad

One of the world's worst nuclear
accidents happened at Chernobyl, in the
Ukraine, in 1986. Radioactive material
spread thousands of miles over many

KAZAKHSTAN

Volga River

Caspian Sea

Volgograd

Cossack dancers

oil

AZERBAIJAN

Caucasus Mountains

Tbilisi

GEORGIA

ARMENIA

Yerevan

Trabzon

otter

Black Sea

Crimea

Sevastopol

The Bosphorus and Dardanelles link the Black Sea to the Mediterranean.

sturgeon

The Bosphorus

Samsun

red deer

Lake Van

grapes

cotton

SYRIA

Damascus

Ankara

Hagia Sofia

TURKEY

Konya

Adana

Taurus Mountains

CYPRUS (Greece, Turkey)

Nicosia

Cyprus has been split into two parts since a war in the 1960s. The north is ruled by people loyal to Turkey and the south is ruled by people loyal to Greece.

Rhodes (Greece)

olive tree

Izmir

Istanbul

The Dardanelles

Pripet Marshes

Chernobyl

Kiev

UKRAINE

Donetsk

Dnieper River

wild boar

Lvov

MOLDOVA

Chisinau

Odesa

oil

Transylvanian Alps

Vlad Dracul's castle

ROMANIA

Bucharest

Danube River

grapes

SERBIA

Belgrade

KOSOVO

Pristina

BULGARIA

Sofia

Skopje

Thessaloniki

olive tree

GREECE

Athens

Parthenon

Crete (Greece)

Iraklion

Mediterranean Sea

POLAND

Warsaw

Some European countries were ruled by Soviet Russia for many years. All are now independent.

Prague

Krakow

CZECH REP.

SLOVAKIA

Bratislava

Vienna

AUSTRIA

Budapest

HUNGARY

SLOVENIA

Ljubljana

Zagreb

CROATIA

Sarajevo

BOSNIA-HERZEGOVINA

Podgorica

MONTENEGRO

Tirana

ALBANIA

MACEDONIA

ITALY

Eurasia

Eurasia includes parts of Europe and Asia. Russia stretches right across it, and is the biggest country in the world.

Arctic Circle

Franz Josef Lan (Russia)

ARCTIC OCEAN

Barents Sea

harp seal

arctic char

Murmansk

Kola Peninsula

Novaya Zemlya (Russia)

Kara Sea

FINLAND

Helsinki

WHITE SEA

Arkhangelsk

eider duck

lemming

wild boar

St Petersburg

BELARUS

Minsk

St Basil's Cathedral

white-tailed eagle

RUSSIA

West of the Ural Mountains, Russia is considered to be in Europe. East of the Urals, it is in Asia.

Kiev

UKRAINE

Moscow

Nizhniy Novgorod

Ob River

Ural Mountains

osprey

Russia has vast areas of open grassland called steppe.

Donetsk

wheat harvest

Kazan

Perm

Volga River

Samara

Ufa

Rostov

Volgograd

Chelyabinsk

Yekaterinburg

Mount Elbrus

flamingo

ibex

Omsk

Tomsk

GEORGIA

Atyrau

saiga

Astrakhan

Tbilisi

sturgeon

oil

KAZAKHSTAN

Novosibirsk

Yerevan

Actau

Aral Sea

Astana

Baikonur Cosmodrome

yak

Caspian Sea

Baku

white pelican

Qaraghandy

A cosmodrome is a space rocket launch site. A cosmonaut is the Russian word for an astronaut.

AZERBAIJAN

cotton

Lake Balkhash

ARMENIA

Tehran

TURKMENISTAN

UZBEKISTAN

Almaty

CHINA

IRAN

Ashgabat

Tashkent

TAJIKISTAN

Bishkek

Samarqand

KYRGYZSTAN

Urumqi

30

Dashanbe

Some of the smaller countries below Russia, such as Kazakhstan and Turkmenistan, were part of the Soviet Union until the early 1990s, when they became independent. The Soviet Union was ruled by Russia.

Wrangel Island (Russia)

Arctic Circle

right whale

Severnaya Zemlya (Russia)

New Siberian Islands (Russia)

Arctic fox

Taymyr Peninsula

Laptev Sea

snowy owl

walrus

Lena River

reindeer

Kamchatka Peninsula

volcanoes

Magadan

pika

Petropavlovsk-Kamchatskiy

elk

raccoon dog

oil

sea otter

Sea of Okhotsk

Kuril Islands (Russia)

Siberia, in Russia, has vast areas of forest called taiga.

Sakhalin (Russia)

brown bear

RUSSIA

Lake Baikal is 5,710 ft deep. It is the deepest lake in the world and contains one fifth of the world's fresh water.

The Trans-Siberian railroad goes from Moscow to Vladivostok, a distance of 5,782 miles.

Yuzhno Sakhalinsk

Bratsk

Eurasian lynx

Khabarovsk

Lake Baikal

Chita

Siberian tiger

Japanese crane

Irkutsk

Ulan Ude

Qiqihar

Vladivostok

Ulan Bator

Harbin

Sea of Japan

JAPAN

MONGOLIA

ger

CHINA

giant octopus

dhole

long-eared jerboa

Shenyang

Tokyo

Beijing

Middle East and Western Asia

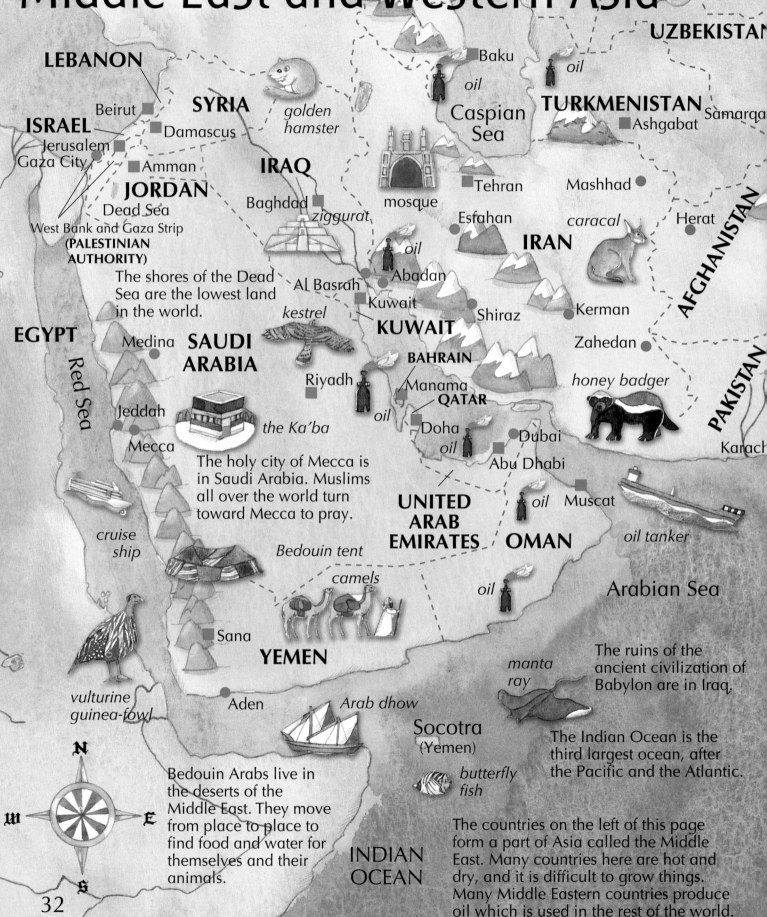

UZBEKISTAN

LEBANON

Baku

oil

oil

Beirut

SYRIA

golden
hamster

TURKMENISTAN
Samarqa

ISRAEL

Damascus

Ashgabat

Jerusalem

IRAQ

mosque

Tehran

Mashhad

Gaza City

Amman

caracal

Herat

JORDAN

Baghdad

Esfahan

Dead Sea

ziggurat

IRAN

West Bank and Gaza Strip
(PALESTINIAN
AUTHORITY)

oil

Abadan

The shores of the Dead
Sea are the lowest land
in the world.

Al Basrah

Kuwait

Shiraz

Kerman

EGYPT

kestrel

KUWAIT

Zahedan

Medina

SAUDI
ARABIA

BAHRAIN

honey badger

Red Sea

Riyadh

Manama

QATAR

oil

Jeddah

the Ka'ba

Doha

Dubai

Mecca

oil

Abu Dhabi

Karach

The holy city of Mecca is
in Saudi Arabia. Muslims
all over the world turn
toward Mecca to pray.

cruise
ship

UNITED
ARAB
EMIRATES

OMAN

oil

Muscat

oil tanker

Bedouin tent

Arabian Sea

camels

oil

Sana

YEMEN

manta
ray

The ruins of the
ancient civilization of
Babylon are in Iraq.

vulturine
guinea-fowl

Aden

Arab dhow

Socotra
(Yemen)

The Indian Ocean is the
third largest ocean, after
the Pacific and the Atlantic.

N

butterfly
fish

Bedouin Arabs live in
the deserts of the
Middle East. They move
from place to place to
find food and water for
themselves and their
animals.

W   E

S

INDIAN
OCEAN

The countries on the left of this page
form a part of Asia called the Middle
East. Many countries here are hot and
dry, and it is difficult to grow things.
Many Middle Eastern countries produce
oil which is used in the rest of the world.

32

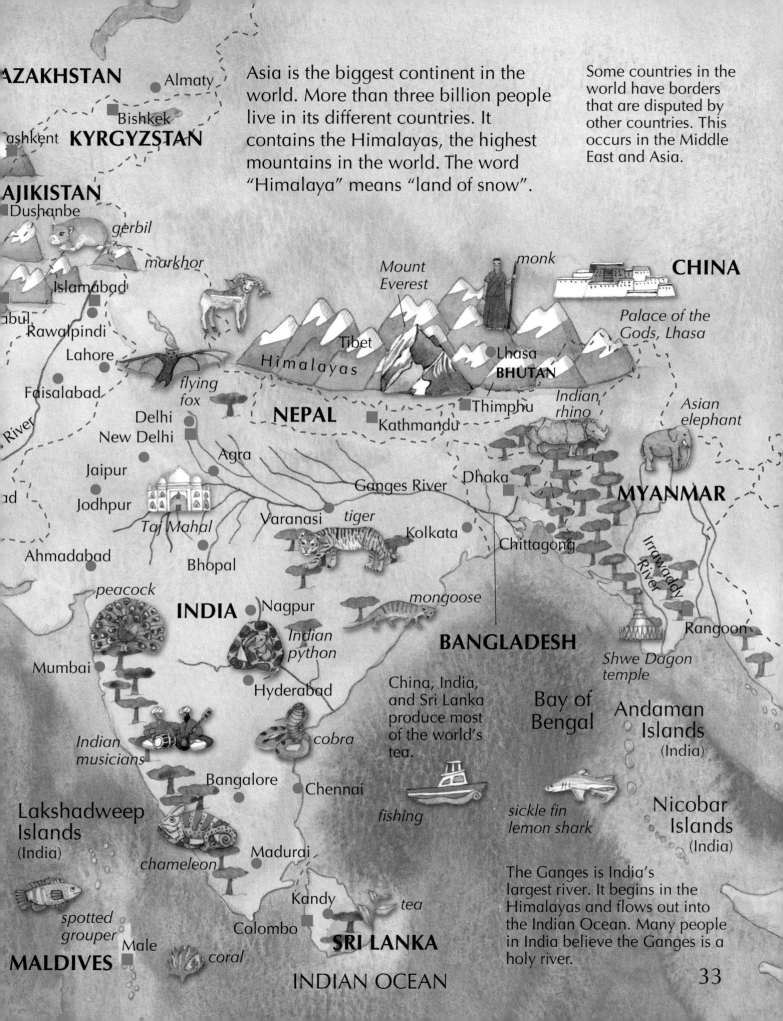

AZAKHSTAN • Almaty

■ Bishkek
ashkent **KYRGYZSTAN**

AJIKISTAN
■ Dushanbe
gerbil

markhor

Asia is the biggest continent in the world. More than three billion people live in its different countries. It contains the Himalayas, the highest mountains in the world. The word "Himalaya" means "land of snow".

Some countries in the world have borders that are disputed by other countries. This occurs in the Middle East and Asia.

Mount Everest

monk

CHINA

■ Islamabad

abul
Rawalpindi
Lahore
Faisalabad

flying fox

Tibet

Lhasa
BHUTAN

Palace of the Gods, Lhasa

Himalayas

■ Thimphu

Indian rhino

Asian elephant

River

Delhi
New Delhi

NEPAL
■ Kathmandu

Jaipur

Agra

Ganges River

Dhaka ■

MYANMAR

ud

Jodhpur

Taj Mahal

Varanasi

tiger

Kolkata

Chittagong

Irrawaddy River

Ahmadabad

Bhopal

peacock

INDIA • Nagpur

Indian python

mongoose

BANGLADESH

Rangoon

Shwe Dagon temple

Mumbai

Hyderabad

China, India, and Sri Lanka produce most of the world's tea.

Bay of Bengal

Andaman Islands (India)

Indian musicians

cobra

Bangalore

Chennai

fishing

sickle fin lemon shark

Nicobar Islands (India)

Lakshadweep Islands (India)

chameleon

Madurai

spotted grouper

Kandy

tea

The Ganges is India's largest river. It begins in the Himalayas and flows out into the Indian Ocean. Many people in India believe the Ganges is a holy river.

■ Male
Colombo

coral

SRI LANKA

MALDIVES

INDIAN OCEAN

33

Southeast Asia

China is part of Southeast Asia, along with many island nations. Over a billion people live in China, more than in any other country in the world.

The Huang Ho (Yellow River) and the Yangtze Kiang are the two great rivers of China. They have been used for hundreds of years to transport people and merchandise all over the country.

The Great Wall of China was built more than two thousand years ago. It is 1,490 miles long.

Japan is a group of long narrow islands. Its highest mountain is the volcano, Mount Fuji.

KAZAKHSTAN

Almaty

otter

RUSSIA

Irkutsk

muskrat

MONGOLIA

Ulan Bator

mountain hare

Ulan-Ude

Lake Baikal
seal

Amur River

Siberian tiger

Khabarovsk

Qiqihar

Harbin

Changchun

Shenyang

Vladivostock

NORTH KOREA

Pyongyang

Seoul

SOUTH KOREA

JAPAN

Sapporo

bullet train

Mount Fuji

Tokyo

Kyoto

Osaka

Kobe

Hiroshima

Nagasaki

traditional dress

tiger shark

Taipei 101, in Taiwan, is the tallest occupied building in the world. It is 1,668 ft tall.

Urumqi

Gobi Desert

wild horses

Hotan

silk moth

snow leopard

CHINA

Temple of Heaven

Baotou

Great Wall of China

Beijing

Tianjin

Terracotta Army

Huang Ho

Shanghai

Wuhan

golden pheasant

Yangtze Kiang

Chinese space center

Chongqing

Guiyang

Kunming

Guangzhou

Taipei

TAIWAN

lesser panda

giant panda

sun bear

NEPAL

Kathmandu

BHUTAN

Thimphu

BANGLADESH

Dhaka

INDIA

Kolkata

Sakhalin
(Russia)

Northern Mariana Islands (US)

PACIFIC OCEAN

Chinese junk

puffer fish

angel fish

green turtle

Equator

PHILIPPINES

mudskipper

PALAU
■ Koror

Manila

Davao

bird of paradise

New Guinea

lion fish

dugong

EAST TIMOR

AUSTRALIA

komodo dragon

praying mantis

Hong Kong is a tiny, overcrowded island off the coast of China. It was ruled by Britain until 1997, when it became part of China. Lots of people from all over the world live and work there, making it an interesting mix of east and west.

South China Sea

(China)

VIETNAM

LAOS

CAMBODIA

Ho Chi Minh City

BRUNEI

flying lemur

Bandar Seri Begawan

orangutan

Ambon

Celebes

INDONESIA

Surabaya

Southeast Asian countries manufacture clothes and other merchandise for countries around the world.

THAILAND

Bangkok

Angkor Wat

Phnom Penh

Gulf of Thailand

MALAYSIA

Kuala Lumpur

Singapore

proboscis monkey

Borneo

Bandung

Java

Jakarta

Christmas Island (Australia)

sea dragon

Bay of Bengal Rangoon

Andaman Islands (India)

Nicobar Islands (India)

slow loris

tarantula spider

Medan

Sumatra

Malayan tapir

killer whale

Javan rhino

Cocos Islands (Australia)

INDIAN OCEAN

The monsoon is a wind that starts in the Indian Ocean and brings very heavy rain to parts of southern Asia during the rainy season. Very little rain falls at other times of the year.

There are thousands of islands off the tip of Asia. Many of them make up countries such as the Philippines and Indonesia. There are over 3,000 islands in Indonesia.

N
E
W
S

North Africa

N W E S

Southern Europe

sardines

Algiers

Tunis

TUNISIA

Tangier

Fès

Oran

date palms

Rabat

Casablanca

MOROCCO

Marrakech

Atlas Mountains

Agadir

underground houses

Tripoli

Funchal

Madeira (Portugal)

The Sahara is the biggest desert in the world. The highest temperature ever was recorded here (135.9° F). Wandering tribes called nomads live here.

oil

Canary Islands (Spain)

Las Palmas

Santa Cruz de Tenerife

Laayoune

In Salah

fennec fox

WESTERN SAHARA

sun fish

MAURITANIA

Sahara Desert

ALGERIA

camels

caracal

spotted hyena

mud-brick buildings

Nouakchott

flamingo

NIGER

Agadèz

Timbuktu

Niger River

Dakar

Senegal River

MALI

SENEGAL

Banjul

Bamako

BURKINA FASO

Niamey

Kano

Ndjamena

Bissau

GUINEA

Ouagadougou

Maiduguri

Conakry

pygmy hippo

gold and diamonds

BENIN

NIGERIA

Abuja

Freetown

Ibadan

Yamoussoukro

Lake Volta

Lagos

leopard

GUINEA BISSAU

Monrovia

IVORY COAST

Porto Novo

Lomé

CAMEROON

GAMBIA

SIERRA LEONE

Abidjan

Accra

Port Harcourt

Yaoundé

LIBERIA

GHANA

TOGO

oil

EQUATORIAL GUINEA

Libreville

Africa is the second biggest continent in the world. It is made up of 53 countries. It has vast deserts, mountains, savanna (grasslands), and rainforests. Many parts of Africa are hot and dry, making it difficult to grow food.

CONGO

GABON

Brazzaville

36

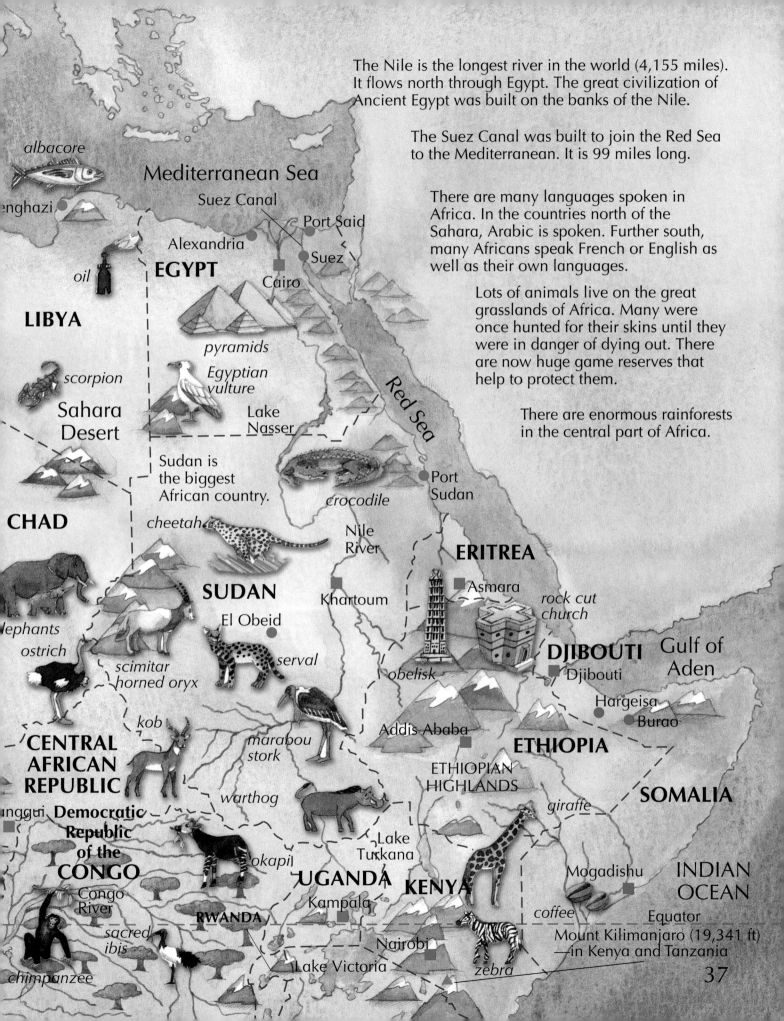

albacore

Mediterranean Sea

Suez Canal

Port Said

Alexandria

EGYPT

Suez

Cairo

enghazi

oil

LIBYA

pyramids

scorpion

Egyptian vulture

Sahara Desert

Lake Nasser

Sudan is the biggest African country.

CHAD

cheetah

crocodile

Port Sudan

Nile River

elephants

ostrich

scimitar horned oryx

SUDAN

El Obeid

serval

Khartoum

ERITREA

Asmara

rock cut church

obelisk

DJIBOUTI

Gulf of Aden

Djibouti

kob

marabou stork

Hargeisa

Burao

CENTRAL AFRICAN REPUBLIC

warthog

Addis Ababa

ETHIOPIA

ETHIOPIAN HIGHLANDS

giraffe

SOMALIA

inggui **Democratic Republic of the CONGO**

okapi

Lake Turkana

Congo River

UGANDA

KENYA

Mogadishu

INDIAN OCEAN

Kampala

coffee

Equator

RWANDA

Mount Kilimanjaro (19,341 ft) —in Kenya and Tanzania

sacred ibis

Nairobi

chimpanzee

Lake Victoria

zebra

The Nile is the longest river in the world (4,155 miles). It flows north through Egypt. The great civilization of Ancient Egypt was built on the banks of the Nile.

The Suez Canal was built to join the Red Sea to the Mediterranean. It is 99 miles long.

There are many languages spoken in Africa. In the countries north of the Sahara, Arabic is spoken. Further south, many Africans speak French or English as well as their own languages.

Lots of animals live on the great grasslands of Africa. Many were once hunted for their skins until they were in danger of dying out. There are now huge game reserves that help to protect them.

There are enormous rainforests in the central part of Africa.

Red Sea

37

Southern Africa

Much of Southern Africa is high, flat grassland. There are also deserts and mountains, and large deposits of gold, diamonds, copper, and tin.

The Zaire River is one of the longest in the world. It flows through thick jungle and is a highway for the people who live in central Africa.

Many African countries used to be run by European countries. Now most are independent, which means they run themselves.

There are water holes in the hot dry grasslands of Africa. Without these, the people and animals who live there would not survive.

Parts of central and southern Africa were first charted by the Scottish explorer, David Livingstone. He was the first outsider to discover the Victoria Falls. He died on his travels in 1873.

Nelson Mandela fought for the rights of black people in South Africa. After spending 28 years in prison on Robben Island, he became the country's first freely elected president in 1994.

The tip of Africa is called the Cape of Good Hope. It is one of the most dangerous shipping routes in the world.

38

green turtle

Portuguese man-of-war jellyfish

ATLANTIC OCEAN

St Helena (UK)

Bata
Libreville
EQUATORIAL GUINEA
Congo River
GABON
Mbandaka
mandrill
CONGO
Democratic Republic of the CONGO
Brazzaville
Kinshasa
Pointe-Noire
Kikwit
Kananga
Mbuji-May
Cabinda (Angola)
Luanda
golden oriol
oil
Lobito
ANGOLA
secretary bird
hoopoe
Namibe
meerka
elephant
porcupine
Windhoek
BOTSWAN
NAMIBIA
Kalahari Desert
fiddler crab
shaft-tailed whydah
gnu
Kimberley
diamonds
springbok
SOUTH AFRICA
Robben Island
Cape Town
Cape of Good Hope
Table Mountain
Cape Agulhas
great white sh

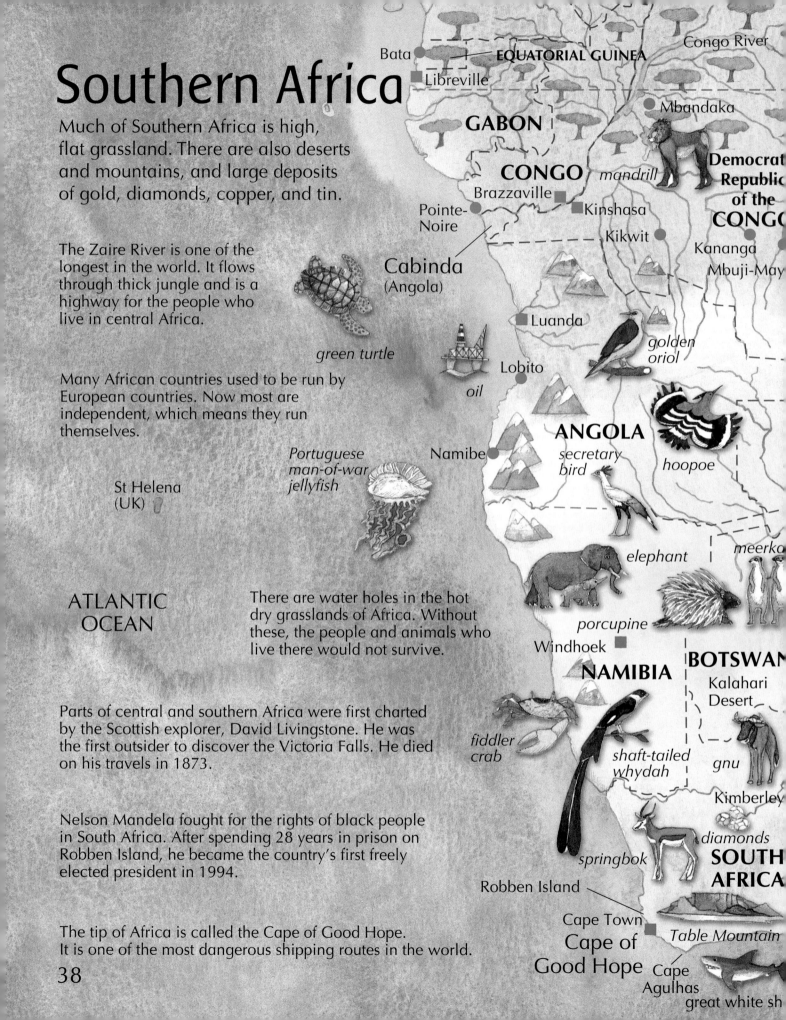

UGANDA
Kampala
gorilla
KENYA
SOMALIA
Mogadishu
Equator
RWANDA
Kigali
Nairobi
Mount Kilimanjaro (19,341 ft)
Lake Victoria
Bujumbura
BURUNDI
Lake Tanganyika
Dodoma
rhino
Mombasa
Zanzibar
Dar es Salaam
giraffe
SEYCHELLES
Victoria

Lake Victoria is the world's second largest freshwater lake, measuring 26,200 sq miles.

Kilimanjaro partly in Tanzania

Aldabra Islands (Seychelles)

INDIAN OCEAN

shoebill
hippo
TANZANIA

Union of COMOROS
Moroni

ulture
lion
fruit bat

Mayotte (France)
Mahajanga
sunbird asity

AMBIA
usaka
Lilongwe
Lake Nyasa
MALAWI
Nacala
Blantyre

stone
ZIMBABWE
Zambezi River
Harare
Victoria Falls
ulawayo
Great Zimbabwe ruins
angolin
Beira
kudu

baobab tree

Antsiranana
Ambilobe

Toamasina
Antananarivo

MADAGASCAR

MAURITIUS
Port Louis
St Denis
Réunion (France)

MOZAMBIQUE
Morombe
Toliara
ring-tailed lemur

Gaborone
Pretoria
Maputo
weto
Mbabane
Johannesburg
SWAZILAND
Maseru
Durban
LESOTHO
gold
Bloemfontein
East London
Port Elizabeth
fin whale

Madagascar is one of the biggest islands in the world. It is the only place, apart from the Comoros, where lemurs live in the wild.

The Victoria Falls is the world's widest waterfall, at roughly 1 mile wide. Local people call it "mosi-oa-tunya", meaning "the smoke that thunders."

There are many different native African peoples and many languages. For instance, the Zulus and the Xhosa people live in South Africa. The Xhosa people use tongue clicks as part of their language.

manta ray

MOZAMBIQUE CHANNEL

N
W
E
S

Australasia and Oceania

The sea over the Marianas Trench is the deepest in the world.

Northern Mariana Islands (US)

Saipan

Guam

Truk Atoll

Palik

PALAU
Koror

lion fish

FEDERATED STATES OF MICRONESIA

Equator

New Guinea

rainbow lorikeet

PAPUA NEW GUINEA

cassowary

Port Moresby

Honiara

sea dragon

Timor Sea

Gulf of Carpentaria

butterfly fish

Coral Sea

INDIAN OCEAN

Darwin

Cairns

Great Barrier Reef

blue damselfis

Australasia is the smallest continent in the world. It includes Australia, New Zealand, and many other island nations.

emu

sulfur-crested cockatoo

AUSTRALIA
aborigine

Mount Isa

Dampier

Great Sandy Desert

Alice Springs

koala

coral

frilled lizard

Uluru

Simpson Desert

Brisbane

Kalgoorlie-Boulder

Great Victoria Desert

Broken Hill

Sydney Opera House

Lord How Island (Australia)

Perth

kangaroo

Adelaide

Sydney

Canberra

surfing

Fremantle

Great Australian Bight

wombat

platypus

Tasmar Sea

Uluru (also called Ayers Rock) is the biggest single rock in the world. It is marked with ancient paintings and carvings, made by the Aborigines, the first people in Australia.

Melbourne

Tasmanian devil

Tasmania

Hobart

humpback whale

great white shark

The desert of northern Australia is often called the "Outback." It is a difficult place to live, since there is very little food or water to find.

The Great Barrier Reef stretches for 1,250 miles in shallow sea off the coast of Australia. It is made of coral with beautiful patterns and colors. The coral was produced by tiny creatures called coral polyps. Lots of sea creatures live on the reef.

Micronesia is made up of 607 small islands.

An atoll is a group of islands around an area of shallow water. They are made from coral which has grown around underwater volcanoes.

Gilbert Islands

Honolulu

Hawaii (US)

Hawaiian dancer

There are thousands of tiny islands in the Pacific near Australia. Many island groups are now independent, but some still belong to the US, Great Britain, France, or other countries.

Bikini Atoll

Marshall Islands

Majuro

manta ray

bottlenose dolphin

Bairiki

PACIFIC OCEAN

Nauru

cruise ship

Equator

KIRIBATI

Tokelau (NZ)

American Samoa (US)

barracuda

olomon Islands

Fongafale

Marquesas Islands

TUVALU

SAMOA

clown fish

VANUATU

Wallis & Futuna (France)

Apia

Cook Islands (NZ)

FRENCH POLYNESIA (France)

Port-Vila

Suva

TONGA

Society Islands

Papeete

bananas

FIJI

Nuku'alofa

Niue (NZ)

Tahiti

New Caledonia (France)

Noumea

Kermadec Islands (NZ)

parrot fish

flying fish

Kingston

Norfolk Island (Australia)

octopus

Some Pacific islands are so densely covered in trees that no humans have ever lived there.

yacht

Pitcairn Islands (UK)

NEW ZEALAND

Auckland

New Zealand has two main islands—North and South Island. There are lots of volcanoes on North Island, along with hot water springs called geysers.

container ship

kiwi

geyser

Maori

Wellington

Christchurch

Chatham Islands (New Zealand)

sheep

Dunedin

albatross

blue whale

Stewart Island

Bounty Islands (New Zealand)

Antipodes Islands (New Zealand)

Auckland Islands (New Zealand)

sperm whale

Campbell Island (New Zealand)

41

The Exploring Game

Imagine that you are an explorer traveling the world, looking for amazing creatures and places. Whenever you want to play the exploring game, pick some pictures shown below and search for them on the maps in this book. Find the answers on page 45.

Two orangutans

Two kiwi birds

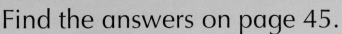
Two igloos

Four albatross birds

An alligator

A chipmunk

A totem pole

A spectacled owl

An iguana

A pirate flag

A manatee

Two leopard seals

Three great white sharks

Four blue whales

Two octopuses

A bull chasing a man

A golden eagle

Two sturgeon fishes

A Cossack dancer

A saiga

A sunfish

A zebra

A spotted hyena

A pair of meerkats

A flying fox

A chameleon

A puffer fish

A tarantula spider

A koala bear

Two sea dragons

43

Glossary

Antarctic Circle
An imaginary circle drawn around the far south of the world.

Arctic Circle
An imaginary circle drawn around the far north of the world.

Atmosphere
A layer of air wrapped around the world. It contains the oxygen we need to breathe.

Capital city
The main city in a country, where the government of the country has its base.

Compass (on a map)
A symbol on a map, marked with the directions of north, south, east, and west.

Continent
The seven main areas of land in the world—North America, South America, Europe, Asia, Australasia, Africa, and Antarctica.

Core
The center of the Earth, made up of incredibly hot metal and rock.

Country
An area of land that has its own government, citizens, and boundaries.

Crust
A layer of rock around the surface of the Earth.

Current
Water flowing in one direction, in an ocean or a river.

Desert
An area of land where there is very little or no water.

Earthquake
When two of the Earth's plates move slightly against each other. This causes the Earth's surface to shudder and sometimes to split.

Equator
An imaginary line around the middle of the Earth.

Grassland
An area of land where most of the plants are grass.

Hurricane
A strong wind that can do lots of damage.

Magma

Molten (very hot) rock beneath the Earth's crust. Sometimes magma comes up to the surface through volcanoes.

Mantle

A layer beneath the Earth's crust, made up of magma (very hot rock).

Monsoon

A wind that blows across Asia at certain times of the year, bringing heavy rains.

North Pole

The point at the far north of the Earth.

Plates

Giant pieces of rock that make up the Earth's crust. They fit together rather like a jigsaw.

Rain forest

A jungle in an area of the world where there is a lot of rainfall and hot weather.

South Pole

The point at the far south of the Earth.

Tundra

An area of land where it is so cold that few plants can grow. Tundra is found near the Arctic and Antarctic Circles.

WEBLINKS

http://www.bbc.co.uk/nature/animals/
Includes live webcams from around the world, with lots of animal features, quizzes, and activities.

http://www.earthcamforkids.com
See lots of images from live webcams all over the world, including famous places, animals, and space.

http://www.earth.nasa.gov/
A site run by space experts, NASA. You can see lots of up-to-the-minute satellite pictures of Earth beamed from space.

http://www.nationalgeographic.com
National Geographic have a kids' section on their website, which includes games and facts about the Earth. Try out their amazing map machine, too. Click on "kids" in the site index.

Answers to game: Orangutans p15, 35. Kiwi birds p15, 41. Igloos p16,19. Albatrosses p14, 17, 25, 41. Totem pole p18. Alligator p21, Chipmunk p21, Spectacled owl p22, Iguana p22, Pirate flag p23. Manatee p24, Leopard seals p17, 25. great white shark p15, 38, 40. Blue whales p14, 17, 25, 41. Octopuses p27, 31. Bull chasing a man p27. Golden eagle p26. Sturgeons p29, 30. Cossack dancer p29. Saiga p30. Sun fish p36. Zebra p37. Spotted hyena p36. Meerkats p38. Flying fox p33. Chameleon p33. Puffer fish p35. Sea dragons p35, 40. Tarantula spider p35. Koala bear p40.

Index